Five GOLDEN RINGS

The Significance of the Five Women in the Genealogy of Jesus

Dr. Charles Dyer

DISPENSATIONAL
PUBLISHING HOUSE, INC.

Copyright © 2017 Charles Dyer
Cover: Leonardo Costa
Illustration: Marcus Nati
Cover and Illustrations © 2017 Dispensational Publishing House, Inc.

All rights reserved. This book or any portion thereof may not be reproduced or used in any manner whatsoever without the express written permission of the publisher except for the use of brief quotations in a book review.

All Scripture quotations, unless otherwise indicated,
are taken from the New American Standard Bible® (NASB),
Copyright © 1960, 1962, 1963, 1968, 1971, 1972, 1973, 1975, 1977, 1995
by The Lockman Foundation
Used by permission. (www.Lockman.org)

Scripture quotations marked (NKJV) are taken from the New King James Version®. Copyright © 1982 by Thomas Nelson. Used by permission. All rights reserved.

Printed in the United States of America

First Edition, First Printing, 2017

ISBN: 978-1-945774-16-4

Dispensational Publishing House, Inc.
PO Box 3181
Taos, NM 87571

www.dispensationalpublishing.com

Ordering Information:
Quantity sales. Special discounts are available on quantity purchases by churches, associations, and others. For details, contact the publisher at the address above.

Orders by U.S. trade bookstores and wholesalers. Please contact the publisher:
Tel: (844) 321-4202

1 2 3 4 5 6 7 8 9 10

This book is dedicated to Cheri Fitzsimmons, Barb Lyon, Jenifer Mason, Margaret Riedel and Nancy Sturges…five of the "golden rings" who have meant so much to Kathy and me over the years. Each one proved to be a blessing in her own unique way. And for that we are deeply grateful!

Table of Contents

The Importance Of People 1

Chapter 1: Tamar 7

Chapter 2: Rahab 17

Chapter 3: Ruth 27

Chapter 4: Bathsheba 39

Chapter 5: Mary 49

Conclusion 61

FOREWORD

THE IMPORTANCE
OF PEOPLE

"If I can't see it, I can't understand it."
—*Albert Einstein*

We understand truth far better when we see it lived out in the lives of others.

For some reason, seeing real flesh-and-blood examples moves truth from the intangible to the tangible . . . from the abstract to the concrete . . . from the theoretical to the practical. Paul understood this when he encouraged the Christians in Corinth to, "Be imitators of me, just as I also am of Christ" (1 Cor. 11:1).

Matthew, the writer of the first book in the New Testament, also understood the importance of wrapping bones and sinew around truth so others could see what it looks like up close and personal. He painted a majestic portrait of Jesus, awash in bright colors and vivid details, showing Him to be "Jesus the Messiah, the son of David, the son of Abraham" (Matt. 1:1).

Matthew began his portrait by taking his readers to ancestry.com . . . tracing the genealogy of Jesus all the way back to Abraham. Sadly, most people do not know what to do when they bump against such a grocery list of names. So they usually just skip over it. After all, many of the names are hard to pronounce, and are not really that significant for readers today ... or are they?

God thought they were important enough to have Matthew start his portrait of Christ by including them.

Perhaps the best approach to this list of names is to begin by asking a different question. What was Matthew's purpose for including such a detailed genealogy? Part of the answer can be found by looking at the women Matthew chose to include in his list. Family identity was normally traced through one's father, and as a result most ancient genealogies focused on the men. There were times when wives or daughters were named, but these were the exception and not the rule. And yet Matthew paused five times in his genealogy to identify specific women who were part of the line of Jesus.

Let us examine that number in its larger context. Matthew linked together 41 men in a human chain stretching from Abraham to Jesus, and we know that each of these men was married. But of all the wives and mothers he could have included, Matthew highlighted just five in his list. He did not include such notable women as Sarah ... or Rebekah ... or Leah. So what is it about the five women Matthew chose that makes them so important to his genealogy? Who are these *Five Golden Rings* in the chain stretching from Abraham to Jesus?

Simply put, that is the focus of this book. Join me on a journey of discovery to explore the five wives and mothers whom Matthew included in his genealogy of Jesus. As we explore each of the five, I believe you will come to understand the special place they play in Matthew's presentation of Jesus as "the Messiah, the son of David, the son of Abraham" (Matt. 1:1).

So let us begin our study of these *Five Golden Rings* in Matthew's genealogy.

CHAPTER 1
Tamar

"Judah was the father of Perez and Zerah by Tamar." (Matt. 1:3)

The first woman named by Matthew in his genealogy of Jesus is Tamar, and she is also almost certainly the least known of the five.

Three different women in the Bible were named Tamar . . . and all experienced sadness and tragedy. One was the daughter of David who was sexually assaulted by her own brother (see 2 Sam. 13:7–14). The second was the daughter of Absalom (see 2 Sam. 14:27)—the son of David who died leading a rebellion against his own father. But the Tamar in Matthew's genealogy lived eight centuries earlier and is the first woman named Tamar in the Bible. She also experienced a difficult life, having been widowed twice. But I am getting ahead of myself, so let us start with Matthew's statement about her in Matthew 1:3: "Judah was the father of Perez and Zerah by Tamar."

The statement seems fairly straightforward, but to understand how Tamar made her way into the genealogy of Jesus we need to travel back to Genesis 38. This chapter records a series of events in the life of Judah, and it is inserted right into the middle of the account of Joseph being taken to Egypt. In fact, it interrupts that narrative. The end of Genesis 37 and the beginning of Genesis 39 fit together perfectly without chapter 38. So why is this chapter in the Bible—and why did God insert it at this exact spot?

Genesis 38 begins with a startling statement. "And it came about at that time, that Judah departed from his brothers" (v. 1). Right into the middle of the account of Joseph being carried off to Egypt is a statement that the line of Abraham, Isaac and Jacob was starting to disintegrate. And the problems seemed to go from bad to worse. In the very next verse, "Judah saw there a daughter of a certain Canaanite whose name was Shua; and he took her and went in to her." Judah not only left his brothers, he married a

Canaanite. His self-serving actions put the entire line of promise in danger. The marriage resulted in three sons—Er, Onan and Shelah. And as Shelah was born we find Judah living in the village of Chezib, called elsewhere Aczib. It is a town in the western foothills near the Elah Valley, where David later fought Goliath (see 1 Sam. 17:2).

And it is at this point in the story of Judah and his family that Tamar enters the picture. As Judah's sons grew, Judah married his oldest to a woman named Tamar. We are not told anything about her background, but from the passage we can assume she was also a Canaanite. In addition to Chezib, two other towns are identified later in the story that seem to anchor Judah and Tamar to the foothills near the Philistine plain.

In Genesis 38:12–14, Judah was traveling to a town named Timnah, near the mouth of the Sorek Valley, when Tamar intercepted him along the way at Enaim, in the Elah Valley. That town, like Kezib, was also in the valley where David later fought Goliath. This region was occupied by the Canaanites, and that is why it is safe to assume Tamar was also a Canaanite. Perhaps she was even from the same extended family as Judah's wife.

The story of Tamar's marriage is both sordid and sad. She was given in marriage to Judah's firstborn son, Er, but he "was evil in the sight of the Lord, so the Lord took his life" (Gen. 38:7). We are not told what Er did, but his conduct was so detestable that God physically killed him. Tamar was now a widow, and her only hope for protection and support rested with Judah's other sons.

The custom of that day was for the next oldest son to marry his brother's widow to produce offspring who would take the place of the brother who had died. But Onan, the second born, was selfish. He did not want to produce a son who would eventually supplant him as the oldest surviving heir, therefore "he wasted his seed on the ground in order not to give offspring to his brother" (Gen. 38:9).

How did God handle this situation? The next verse tells us:

> But what he did was displeasing in the sight of the LORD; so He took his life also. (Gen. 38:10)

Judah started with three sons, but he was now down to just one. Though he was expected to give his third son to Tamar, he hesitated ... saying this son was too young to marry. But as time went on it became clear Judah had no intention of fulfilling his obligation to Tamar. He had given her two sons, and they were now dead. And with the recent death of his own wife, Judah didn't want to risk the life of his only remaining son and heir by having him marry Tamar.

That is when Tamar took matters into her

own hands. She dressed up as a prostitute and sat by the roadway in the Elah Valley, knowing Judah was about to pass by. He saw her, thought she was a prostitute, and decided to purchase the *sexual services* of this *woman along the way*, not realizing she was his daughter-in-law. He paid for her services using the accepted credit card of the day—his "seal and . . . staff" (v. 18), which were his proof of identity. He left these as a pledge and promised to "send" someone back with "a young goat from the flock" as payment (v. 17). But when Judah sent his friend back, the woman had vanished.

From that one sexual encounter Tamar became pregnant. When Judah found out, he was angry over her obvious unfaithfulness and demanded that she be brought out and put to death for adultery. That is when Tamar produced the "seal and . . . staff" (v. 18) and said, "I am with child by the man to whom these things belong" (v. 25).

Judah recognized immediately his wickedness in not fulfilling his obligation to Tamar. His disregard for her welfare had driven her to take such desperate measures. He sadly reported, "She is more righteous than I" (v. 26). Tamar eventually gave birth to twins who were legally recognized as Judah's sons. And the oldest of the twins, Perez, ended up in the line of David—and Jesus.

But wait! This is supposed to be a wondrous tale of faith and hope . . . a story about the first of the *Five Golden Rings* of Matthew 1. We were expecting a heartwarming story of love, anticipation and promise, and instead we are left shaking our heads as the Bible unflinchingly records this sordid tale of betrayal and immorality. If anything, the story shows the frailness, hubris and propensity for evil that lies at the heart of our human existence. So why would God choose to include this woman in the genealogy of the Savior?

I see two important reasons for including

Tamar in the genealogy. First, I believe God initially included the story of Judah and Tamar in the Bible, even having it interrupt the account of Joseph, to make a point. The promised line was in danger, and Joseph's slavery in Egypt was part of God's plan to rescue that line. As Joseph said later to his brothers, "As for you, you meant evil against me, *but* God meant it for good in order to bring about this present result, to preserve many people alive" (Gen. 50:20).

Second, I believe God included Tamar in the genealogy of Jesus to show how God can even work through the sinful actions of others, like Judah and Tamar, to accomplish His plan of salvation for the world. Tamar is a living illustration of Paul's promise in Romans 8:28 that, "God causes all things to work together for good to those who love God." All things are not good, but God can even use those situations that are evil and wrong to ultimately bring about something good. Remember, in God's larger plan the child of Judah and Tamar ended up producing King David—and Messiah Jesus! Never forget, the God who worked out His plan for the line of David through Judah and Tamar can also make "all things to work together for good" in your life—whatever your circumstances might happen to be!

CHAPTER 2
Rahab

"Salmon was the father of Boaz by Rahab." (Matt. 1:5)

If Tamar seemed like an unusual choice to include in Matthew's *Five Golden Rings* of Christmas, then the second woman in Matthew's list will also raise some eyebrows. Matthew introduces her this way: "Salmon was the father of Boaz by Rahab" (Matt. 1:5).

But before we take a closer look at Rahab, I need to take you back to my hometown to introduce you to some of the people I knew growing up. The first is Dick the Mailman, who delivered our mail. He went to our church, but I do not recall ever hearing his last name. He was just Dick the Mailman. And then there is Joe the Barber. That is the name he went by. He even had it inscribed on his tombstone while he was still alive!

There are people in life who are just known for what they do. Steve Jobs? Apple! Bill Gates? Microsoft! And if I say Rahab, what comes to mind? If you know the Bible, the next word out

of your mouth is her occupation—harlot! Rahab is actually identified by name eight times in the Bible, and in five of the eight she is called a harlot. She is talked about in four different books of the Bible (Joshua, Matthew, Hebrews and James) and the only one not to add the word *harlot* to her name is Matthew.

Now, some have tried to soften the blow to Rahab's reputation by saying she was an *innkeeper* and not a prostitute. The Jewish historian Josephus refers to the spies retiring "to a certain inn that was near the wall" that was "kept by Rahab."[1] Unfortunately, the Hebrew word used to describe Rahab is *harlot* or *prostitute*, and it comes from a word that means "to commit fornication." The Septuagint translation of the Old Testament, along with the books of Hebrews and James in the New Testament, use the word *pornē* to describe Rahab. We get the words *porn* and *pornography* from that word—and it does not refer to an innkeeper.

It is one thing to be known as Dick the Mailman or Joe the Barber. Those are honorable professions. But how would you like to go through life with everyone attaching the word *prostitute* to your name? To put it kindly, Rahab was a woman with baggage. Think about all the disadvantages she faced. She was a Canaanite, not an Israelite. She was a woman in a society that viewed women more as possessions than people. And . . . she was a prostitute. She sold her body

---

[1] Josephus, *Antiquities* 5.1.2.

for the selfish gratification of others.

Jericho straddled a major crossing point into Canaan at the Jordan River. And it stood at the meeting point of three roadways leading up into the mountainous interior. Caravans arriving from the desert or preparing to cross the Jordan on their way to Ammon, Moab, Edom and other points east stopped at Jericho.

Lonely men. Smelly men. Men looking for a good time. And Rahab was the woman whose name was on every restroom wall. "For a good time, contact her!" From a human perspective, Rahab's life looked bleak. She could expect to be used hard and then cast aside when she became too old, or too diseased . . . or when someone younger and fresher came along to take her place.

But circumstances do not determine destiny. One thing set Rahab apart. And we see it in the words she spoke to the spies who came to her in Jericho.

> I know that the LORD has given you the land, and that the terror of you has fallen on us, and that all the inhabitants of the land have melted away before you. For we have heard how the LORD dried up the water of the Red Sea before you when you came out of Egypt, and what you did to the two kings of the Amorites who were beyond the Jordan, to Sihon and Og, whom you utterly destroyed. When we heard *it*, our hearts melted and no courage remained in any man any longer because of you; for the LORD your God, He is God in heaven above and on earth beneath. (Josh. 2:9–11)

How did Rahab know this? She did not have access to the five books of Moses, the only part of the Bible even written at that point. So how could she know anything about the God of Israel? Likely, travelers passing through Jericho—and stopping to use her services—shared bits of news and gossip about what was happening in the region, including reports about a group of people . . . and the God they served . . . and the things that He had done. Rahab did not know much, but she believed—and acted on—the truth she had heard. As the story unfolds, we discover that Rahab was willing to trust her life, and the lives of her loved ones, on a promise made to her in the name of the God of Israel . . . a God she had only heard about secondhand.

Rahab's faith saved her physically, but it did so much more. Because of her willingness to risk her life to protect the two spies, this Canaanite harlot was accepted by the Israelites in spite of her previous background. She ceased being just a mere object and became the beloved wife of Salmon. And Salmon was not some bucktoothed bumpkin who could not get a respectable girl to be his wife. His dad was Nahshon, who happened to be "the leader of the sons of Judah" (Num. 2:3). In fact, Moses put Nahshon in charge of organizing the fighting men from that tribe (Num. 1:3–4, 7)! I cannot prove it, but I wonder if Salmon might not have been one of the two spies sent on that daring mission into Jericho by Joshua. It is at least possible.

But we are not through with Rahab's continuing impact. Rahab gave birth to a son who would play a major role in Israel's transformation into a nation. His name was Boaz. I could say more about him, but that is a subject for our next chapter. And ultimately, through that son, Rahab became a link in the chain that led to both David and Jesus.

And yet, the story of Rahab still is not finished. In the New Testament the writers of both Hebrews and James point to Rahab as a shining example of faith. In fact, Rahab is one of only two women identified by name in the Hebrews 11 *Hall of Faith*. This woman who started out as a prostitute ended up as the mother of kings. And the turning point came when she decided to trust God with her life.

And that brings us back to Matthew 1—to the *Five Golden Rings* in the genealogy of Jesus . . . and to you. I find it fascinating that Matthew is the only author in the Bible who refers to Rahab without calling her a harlot. And I believe he does this for a very important reason. While the other writers were focusing on Rahab's life—which had to include her past—Matthew has a forward focus. He is not looking at where Rahab was from, but where she was going. And that, my friend, may be Rahab's greatest lesson for all of us. You see, from God's eternal perspective it does not matter where you are from, or what you have done. God is infinitely more concerned with who you are . . . and where you are going. And Rahab is a reminder of what God can do with and through a person willing to put his or her faith in Him!

CHAPTER 3
Ruth

"Boaz was the father of Obed by Ruth."
(Matt. 1:5)

We have reached the midpoint in Matthew's *Five Golden Rings*—the five women Matthew included in his genealogy of Jesus. Matthew introduces the third woman this way: "Boaz was the father of Obed by Ruth" (Matt. 1:5).

I find it fascinating that the first three women listed by Matthew in his genealogy share one thing in common. They were not Israelites. That is, they were not physical descendants of Abraham, Isaac and Jacob. Tamar and Rahab were Canaanites, while Ruth was from Moab. The first two lived in the land of Canaan, but Ruth did not even have that geographical connection. The Moabites were distant relatives of the Israelites. The nation sprang from an incestuous relationship between Abraham's nephew Lot and Lot's daughter (see Gen. 19:30-38).

Yet it was not Moab's family history that bothered the children of Israel. Rather, it was Moab's actions near the end of the wilderness wanderings. The Moabites refused to extend any physical help to the thirsty, hungry Israelites (see Judg. 11:17-18). Worse than that, they hired the prophet Balaam to curse the nation (see Num. 22-24). And when that failed, they sent the daughters of Moab to sexually tempt the men of Israel into idolatry, resulting in a plague that killed 24,000 Israelites (see Num. 25:1-9; 1 Cor. 10:8).

With the sting of these actions still fresh on their minds, the command in Deuteronomy 23 prohibiting Moabites from entering the assembly of the LORD seems to make perfect sense.

> No Ammonite or Moabite shall enter the assembly of the LORD; none of their *descendants*, even to the tenth generation, shall ever enter the assembly of the LORD, because they did not meet you with food and water on the way when you came out of Egypt, and because they

> hired against you Balaam the son of Beor from Pethor of Mesopotamia, to curse you. (Deut. 23:3-4)

Some think "the assembly of the LORD" refers to the tabernacle, the place where Israel was to assemble before God in worship. Others think "the assembly" refers to the nation as a whole. We might view it today as being equivalent to citizenship. But whichever is in focus, the Moabites were denied entry. In fact, Deuteronomy 23 concludes by commanding Israel: "You shall never seek their peace or their prosperity all your days" (v. 6).

God announced there would be no entrance for Moabites "even to the tenth generation" (Deut. 23:3). Assuming couples started having children around the age of 20, 10 generations would exclude the descendant of any Moabite for at least 200 years. And some believe the phrase "even to the tenth generation" actually means *forever*, since 10 was often the number of completion.

And that brings us back to Ruth. Though she was the widow of an Israelite, she was still a foreigner—part of a group specifically excluded from the assembly. Surely she knew this before deciding to return to the land of Israel with Naomi. And that is what makes Ruth's affirmation of her commitment to Naomi so remarkable.

> But Ruth said, "Do not urge me to leave you *or* turn back from following you; for where you go, I will go, and where you lodge, I will lodge. Your people *shall be* my people, and your God, my God. Where you die, I will die, and there I will be buried. Thus may the LORD do to me, and worse, if *anything but* death parts you and me." (Ruth 1:16-17)

Ruth had nothing to gain by following Naomi. Naomi had no other son for her to marry. Naomi had nothing of value for Ruth to inherit. Ruth would be an outsider—a detested Moabite no less—in a nation that seemed to offer little hope of acceptance. But Ruth still made a clear-eyed commitment. Naomi's people would be her people . . . and Naomi's God would be her God.

Most people know the story of Ruth and Boaz, but have you ever wondered why Boaz was willing to do so much to help Ruth? We romanticize the event and think perhaps it was because she was so exotic—or young and pretty. But could it be that Boaz took such an interest in Ruth for two entirely different reasons? Certainly he wanted to honor her faithfulness to Naomi (cf. Ruth 2:10–12). And yet, could his actions also stem, at least in part, from his own personal knowledge of how difficult life could be for someone from a different ethnic and social background? Perhaps he thought of his own background . . . and Rahab the Canaanite harlot. It just might be that his family background gave him an additional measure of compassion for this young woman who had made such a strong commitment to the people and God of Israel

We love the end of the story, but we are still left with one troubling question. If no descendants of Moab, "even to the tenth generation" (Deut. 23:3), were to be allowed into the assembly of Israel, then what do we do with the fact that Ruth's great-grandson—a mere three generations away—was David? Actually, there are at least two possible answers.

Some think there could be gaps in the genealogy—so that David was, in fact, 10 generations removed. We do know there are times when individuals are left out of genealogies, with the writers skipping over some of the more minor characters in the account to focus on the more prominent descendants. The fall of Jericho took place around 1405 B.C. and David was born about 1040 B.C., 365 years later. In that 365-year period the only descendants listed are Salmon, Boaz, Obed, Jesse and David. That is about 90 years between the birth of each generation. And while I suppose that is at least possible, it is not very likely. Certainly 365 years easily allows for the birth of up to 10 generations.

Unfortunately, I do not believe this potential solution solves the problem. Even if we assume there is a gap in the genealogy, that gap would likely need to occur between Salmon and Boaz ... not between Boaz and David. The genealogy from Boaz to David seems not to contain any gaps because the exact same sequence of fathers and sons is repeated in Ruth 4:20-22; 1 Chronicles 2:11-15; and Luke 3:31-32. In all these accounts David is still the great-grandson of Boaz—still just three generations removed from Ruth the Moabitess.

There is a second possible explanation. God might have extended special grace to Ruth because of her remarkable statement of faith. She was not the *typical* Moabite. Instead, she renounced her former background and publicly declared her allegiance to the people of Israel, and to their God. "Your people *shall be* my people, and your God, my God" (Ruth 1:16). Several hundred years later the prophet Isaiah described the coming kingdom age as a time when God will extend His blessing to those who were previously thought to be excluded.

> Let not the foreigner who has joined himself to the Lord say,
> "The Lord will surely separate me from His people."
> Nor let the eunuch say, "Behold, I am a dry tree."
>
> For thus says the Lord,
>
> "To the eunuchs who keep My sabbaths,
> And choose what pleases Me,
> And hold fast My covenant,
> To them I will give in My house and within My walls a memorial,
> And a name better than that of sons and

daughters;
I will give them an everlasting name
which will not be cut off.

"Also the foreigners who join themselves to the LORD,
To minister to Him, and to love the name of the LORD,
To be His servants, every one who keeps from profaning the sabbath
And holds fast My covenant;
Even those I will bring to My holy mountain
And make them joyful in My house of prayer.
Their burnt offerings and their sacrifices will be acceptable on My altar;
For My house will be called a house of prayer for all the peoples." (Isa. 56:3-7)

Could Matthew have included Ruth in the genealogy for this very purpose—to remind Israel that Ruth was the first actual example of the blessing God later said would come to all nations during the age of the Messiah? Ruth the foreigner joined herself to the Lord, and God accepted her into His fellowship. More than that, she became another link in the promised line leading to David ... and to Messiah Jesus!

But what does Ruth have to do with us? The truth we can take away from our study of Ruth is this: No matter what a person's family background or history might be, it cannot keep him or her from a relationship with God if that person truly wants to know Him. The God who can reverse a curse placed on a nation is the same God who can undo the chains that handcuff us to our past. But the key to unlocking those chains begins with a commitment to make the God of Israel—the God of the Bible—your God. If you have not done so before, would not this be a wonderful time to begin that journey in your life?

You can do that right now by placing your trust for eternal life on what Jesus Christ has done for you. Do you believe that when Jesus died on the cross, He did so to pay the penalty for your sins? Are you willing to make Him the Lord and Savior of your life? If you are, you can do so by praying a simple prayer like that which follows.

Dear Lord, I know that my life is a mess and that I am separated from you. I also know and believe that you sent your Son, Jesus Christ, to Earth to die on the cross to pay the penalty for my sin. I now want to place my trust in Him as the substitute for my sin. Please forgive me and give me eternal life. In Christ's name I ask this. Just like Ruth of old, I want to make You, and You alone, the God of my life. Amen.

If you just prayed something like this, I have two suggestions for you. First, start reading the Bible. A good place to begin is the gospel of John to learn more about Jesus. Second, find a church that believes and teaches the Bible and start attending there. Invest time in learning more about Jesus!

CHAPTER 4
Bathsheba

*"David the king begot Solomon by
her who had been the wife of Uriah."*
(Matt. 1:6, NKJV)

I grew up in the era of the anonymous hero. Whether it was the Lone Ranger, Superman, Batman or Spiderman, it seemed like every hero felt it was essential to keep his or her true identity secret. And, frankly, some of the disguises they used were pretty lame. A man shows up in a suit and tie wearing glasses. It is Clark Kent! He steps into a storage room and out jumps a man wearing blue tights with a red "S" on the chest . . . and no glasses. It is Superman! Did not anyone notice the physical resemblance between these two men who always seemed to be connected to the same events . . . though never actually being in the same place at the same time?

We have come to the fourth of Matthew's *Five Golden Rings*—the five women he included in his genealogy of Jesus. And it is here where Matthew introduces us to his version of the unknown hero. No, she does not "leap tall buildings in a single bound." But Matthew describes her without ever telling us her name—though it is easy to guess her identity. Here is what he says: "David the king begot Solomon by her *who had been the wife* of Uriah" (Matt. 1:6, NKJV).

So who was the mother of Solomon . . . or the wife of Uriah? It is Bathsheba. We all know the name of this woman with whom David had an affair. So why did Matthew not identify her by name? That is the mystery behind our fourth *golden ring*. It is obvious who the woman in question really is. But if Matthew went out of his way to remind us that Solomon's mother had been the wife of Uriah, why did he not simply state her name? Why hide her identity with a disguise as lame as the glasses on Clark Kent's face?

To answer the question, we need to look more closely at Bathsheba. Bathsheba is the first woman in Matthew's genealogy who was actually an Israelite by birth. While her name can be translated *daughter of Sheba*, we know Sheba was not the name of her father. Second Samuel 11:3 specifically identifies her as "the daughter of Eliam." So it is probably best to understand her name to mean "daughter of the oath" or "daughter of the seven."

We pass over the name of her father Eliam because it means little to us. But most likely this is the same Eliam who is listed as one of David's elite group of warriors, known collectively as "the Thirty." Think of this group as the SEAL Team Six of David's day. Eliam's father was none other than Ahithophel, one of David's two most trusted counselors. In short, Bathsheba is the daughter of an elite warrior, and the granddaughter of one of the royal court's most senior advisors.

But that is not all. When she was first identified to David, the night he saw her bathing on the roof, the messenger added one additional piece of information. Bathsheba was also "the wife of Uriah the Hittite" (2 Sam. 11:3). As a Hittite, Uriah descended from one of the original people groups living in the land of Canaan. But even though he was not a physical descendant of Abraham, he appears to have become a follower of the God of Israel. The *yah* sound at the end of his name comes from the covenant name of God, *Yahweh*. Uriah's name means "my light is the LORD [Yahweh]."

Uriah was more than a mere mercenary soldier, and even more than just a follower of the God of Israel. He is also identified as one of the elite warriors in David's band of 30. He might not have been a native-born Israelite, but he had achieved a position of trust and honor in David's inner circle. And his marriage to Bathsheba suggests he was fully accepted by David and the other members of the royal court.

But we are still faced with our original question. Why did not Matthew identify Bathsheba by name? Thomas Aquinas suggested it was because of her complicity in the sin that marred David's reign. So, he wrote, "Bathsheba was not only consenting in the adultery, but in the murder of her husband, hence her name is not introduced in the Lord's genealogy."[2] But this seems a bit harsh. Bathsheba was by no means an innocent party in the sordid affair that followed, but David was most responsible for what happened. At the end of the chapter we read that "the thing that David had done was evil in the sight of the LORD" (2 Sam. 11:27). And to say Bathsheba was not named because of her sin does not explain why Tamar or Rahab are named, since both committed similar sins.

So, if Bathsheba's name was not omitted to show God's displeasure with her, then what other possible reason could there be? Like the

---

2 Thomas Aquinas, *Catena Aurea*, vol. 1, "St. Matthew," part 1, trans. by John Henry Parker and J. Rivington (London: James Parker and Co., 1874), p. 25.

proverbial elephant in the room, it is obvious Matthew wanted to identify Bathsheba without using her name. But why?

Perhaps the answer can be found not in the name that has been omitted ... but in the one that has been added. Could it be that Matthew is not slighting Bathsheba, but is rather emphasizing Uriah? The first three *golden rings* in Matthew's genealogy—Tamar, Rahab and Ruth—were all women who were not Israelites but who married Israelites, and thus married into the promised line. They were Gentiles. Bathsheba was an Israelite, but her first husband was not. Uriah was a God-fearing Hittite, a man whose name meant "my light is the Lord," a man who followed the God of Israel from his heart—not merely because of his heritage.

Do not get me wrong. I do not believe Matthew is covering up the sin of David and Bathsheba. By stressing the fact that David fathered Solomon through a woman who had been another man's wife, Matthew reminds his readers of the terrible events that overshadowed the first ruler from God's chosen line of kings. But by naming Uriah, and not Bathsheba, Matthew could possibly be reminding us again that the final Son of David will not only be the King of the Jews. He will also be King of all the Earth. It is encouraging to me that Matthew's description of the genealogy of Jesus includes Canaanites, Moabites and Hittites along with the chosen seed from the line of Abraham.

So what truths can we carry away from this *golden ring* in the genealogy of Jesus? I would like to suggest two. First, God cares for everyone in the world. It is exciting to watch Matthew weave together the genealogy of Jesus in a way that includes Gentiles. I spend much time teaching about Israel, and I have a deep love for the Jewish people. But it is also essential to remember that God's love extends to "every tribe and tongue and people and nation," as Revelation 5:9 tells us. If you want a heart that beats in tune with God's, then you need a heart of love for all the people of the world.

Second, this account reminds us that God's grace far surpasses our sin. David's sin with Bathsheba is a story of adultery and murder. And the consequences of that sin resulted in the death of a child, the fracturing of a family and a war that nearly tore apart a nation. And yet God's grace reached into that dark abyss to provide forgiveness for David and Bathsheba ... and ultimately to graciously give them another son, Solomon, through whom the royal line would continue.

I do not know the burden of pain, sorrow or guilt you might be carrying on your shoulders today ... but God does. And God has promised that:

> If we confess our sins, He is faithful and righteous to forgive us our sins and to

cleanse us from all unrighteousness. (1 John 1:9)

Would it not be great to end this day knowing a load of guilt has been lifted off your shoulders? You can experience God's forgiveness right now. Open your Bible to 1 John 1:9 and read the promise God has made to you. It might just be the best gift you receive all year!

CHAPTER 5
Mary

"Jacob was the father of Joseph the husband of Mary, by whom Jesus was born, who is called the Messiah."
(Matt. 1:16)

We have reached the final link in our chain of *Five Golden Rings*—the five women Matthew included in his genealogy of Jesus. And in many ways Mathew has saved the best for last, though his way of introducing Mary seems a bit awkward. Here is what he says: "Jacob was the father of Joseph the husband of Mary, by whom Jesus was born, who is called the Messiah" (Matt. 1:16).

In what way is the wording awkward? Well, for each of the first four women in his list, Matthew used the exact same word order. "And to [the husband] was born [the son] *ek tēs*, which literally means 'out of' or 'from' [the woman]." So he writes:

- "Judah was the father of Perez and Zerah by ['out of/from'] Tamar." (Matt. 1:3)

- "Salmon was the father of Boaz by ['out of/from'] Rahab." (Matt. 1:5)

- "Boaz was the father of Obed by ['out of/

from'] Ruth." (Matt. 1:5)

- "David was the father of Solomon by ['out of/from'] Bathsheba who had been the wife of Uriah ['she of Uriah']." (Matt. 1:6)

But when Matthew gets to the birth of Jesus, the wording changes. He says Joseph was "the husband of Mary, by whom Jesus was born" (Matt. 1:16)—and he uses the feminine pronoun, to let us know he is referring only to Mary. In short, Matthew goes out of his way to stress that Mary was the mother of Jesus while Joseph was not the father—simply the husband of the mother. Matthew later explains why this distinction was necessary. Before Mary and Joseph "came together" in any sort of physical, intimate way, Mary "was found to be with child by the Holy Spirit" (Matt. 1:18). Joseph was the legal father of Jesus, but he was not the biological father.

Of the *Five Golden Rings* in Matthew's

genealogy, Mary seems the most clearly deserving of the honor. After all, she was the physical mother of Jesus. And by quoting Isaiah 7:14 Matthew also lets us know that her pregnancy was a prophetically significant, divine miracle (cf. Matt. 1:22–23).

Sadly, there is a great deal of misunderstanding about Mary. Some have so honored her that they almost suggest she is equal to, or even greater than, the Son she bore. Others have reacted by going in the opposite direction, giving Mary little attention—and almost no honor. It is almost as if they see her as little more than a typical Jewish maiden of the day. She won God's heavenly lottery, and her womb was selected for the Messiah. But they almost suggest there was nothing unusual or special about her that set her apart in any way from the thousands of others God could have chosen. I believe the truth lies somewhere in between ... which means I run the risk of offending nearly everyone reading! So I ask you to please read what I have to say very carefully.

The name Mary in our Bibles is really the Hebrew name *Miriam* ... the same name as that given to Moses' sister (cf. Ex. 15:20). And, no doubt, it was because of Moses' sister that the name seemed to be so popular in Jesus' day. The fact that Mary's parents named her after a beloved prophetess of Israel might suggest their high hopes for their young daughter. But surely Mary exceeded whatever aspirations they might have had at the time of her birth. We can clearly see her godly character shining through in the other gospel account ... that penned by Dr. Luke.

Luke first identified Mary as a chaste woman, a virgin (Luke 1:26–27). But more than that, she was "favored" (v. 28). Lest we miss the point, the angel who appeared to her repeated the statement a few verses later. "Do not be afraid, Mary; for you have found favor with God" (v. 30). The word "favor" comes from *charis*, the Greek word for *grace*. Luke's use of *charis* here reminds me of the description of Noah in the book of Genesis.

In Genesis 6 God announced He would destroy the earth because of humanity's wickedness. But then Moses introduced a man who stood in stark contrast to the rest of the world. "But Noah found favor in the eyes of the Lord" (Gen. 6:8). In the Septuagint translation of the Old Testament, the word for "favor" is *charis*. Noah was different from everyone else in his day, and I believe the angel in Luke 1 is making a similar statement about Mary. She was chosen because she was special.

We see Mary's tender heart and submissive spirit in her response to the angel's announcement. "Behold, the bondslave of the Lord; may it be done to me according to your word" (Luke 1:38). The word for "bondslave" is *doulos*, the

Greek word for a slave. Mary's heart attitude was that of an obedient slave to the will of God. Later, when Mary visited with her relative Elizabeth, she sang a song of praise to God.

> And Mary said:
>
> "My soul exalts the Lord,
> And my spirit has rejoiced in God my Savior.
>
> "For He has had regard for the humble state of His bondslave;
>
> For behold, from this time on all generations will count me blessed." (Luke 1:46–48)

It is important for us all to acknowledge that Mary was obedient, humble and submissive in her actions. She was—and is—a model of faithfulness. But it is Luke who tells us this, not Matthew. Matthew includes Mary in his genealogy but provides little personal information about her. So why did Matthew include Mary in his genealogy?

Let me suggest a possible answer that flows in part from the other women Matthew listed in his genealogy. Matthew recorded five women in the line of Jesus. One had sexual relations with her father-in-law, one was a former prostitute and one committed adultery. The only one who had not committed sexual immorality was Ruth, and she was from a nation despised by the Jewish people. Four women . . . all of whom were flawed by the standards of the day. And for three of them the flaws were related to sexual immorality.

And then we come to Mary. She was sexually pure . . . a virgin. She was "favored" . . . one who lived in a special relationship to God. And then . . . she became pregnant! To fulfill Isaiah's prophecy of a virgin birth (see Isa. 7:14), God needed a virgin, a sexually pure woman not yet in a marriage relationship. But when an unmarried young woman becomes pregnant, especially in that day, questions were raised. No doubt Mary was unjustly accused of being morally impure. At one point, when Jesus was challenged in the temple, His accusers said, "We were not born of fornication" (John 8:41), likely suggesting that they thought He was.

Could Matthew have included all these women in the genealogy of Christ, in part, to help answer the unjust accusations that were hurled against Mary? The genealogy of David was filled with flawed women through whom God worked out His miraculous plan. But when it came to selecting the woman who was to give birth to the Messiah, God chose a chaste, godly woman . . . a woman who, like Noah, stood out from her contemporaries, a woman "highly favored" (Luke 1:28, NKJV) by God. Mary was the one woman in Matthew's genealogy without any past baggage. She was the one qualified to fulfill Isaiah's promise of a virgin birth. And, yet, she was also the one who had to bear the unjust criticism of those who refused to acknowledge the miracle God had brought about in her body.

So what truth can we carry away from the life of Mary? Perhaps it is her example of total devotion to God—a devotion that resulted in ridicule and scorn from those who misunderstood her motives, misinterpreted her circumstances, or missed the very fulfillment of prophecy God brought about in her life. If you want to give your life to God and serve Him wholeheartedly, be prepared to be misunderstood . . . and, at times, even mistreated.

Peter said it this way:

> Beloved, do not be surprised at the fiery ordeal among you, which comes upon you for your testing, as though some strange thing were happening to you; but to the degree that you share the sufferings of Christ, keep on rejoicing, so that also at the revelation of His glory you may rejoice with exultation. If you are

reviled for the name of Christ, you are blessed, because the Spirit of glory and of God rests on you. (1 Pet. 4:12-14)

Mary was *favored* ... and Peter says we can be blessed. Mary experienced the Holy Spirit overshadowing her (see Luke 1:35) ... and Peter says we have "the Spirit of glory" resting on us. But in spite of all that, Mary had to endure the taunts of others who did not understand what God had done ... and Peter says there are times when we will also endure such painful trials. And, in that sense, Mary is a fitting way to end our study of the *Five Golden Rings* in Mathew's genealogy. She is a great example of what it means to be faithful ... no matter what obstacles we might face.

CHAPTER 6

Conclusion

"And we know that God causes all things to work together for good to those who love God, to those who are called according to His purpose." (Rom. 8:28)

We have completed our study of the *Five Golden Rings*—the five unique women who together help forge the human chain stretching from Abraham, through David, to Jesus. But what is the *takeaway* from our study? What life lessons from these five women can we stuff into our backpack to help us make our way through this journey we call life?

I see five realities of life illustrated in the lives of these women ... five truths we can mine from Matthew's genealogy.

Tamar reminds us that "God causes all things to work together for good" (Rom. 8:28) ... even when those circumstances and events might not, by themselves, *be good*. God used Joseph to save the line of Abraham in spite of Judah's poor life choices (see Gen. 50:20). And God was able to override the sin of Tamar and Judah to preserve the promised line. What they did was wrong, but God superintended through it all to produce a son who would provide the link to David and Jesus.

No matter what the problem, always remember that God is in control. You can trust Him, even when the things you are experiencing seem neither fair nor right.

Rahab reminds us that God is more concerned with where we are going than where we have been. We cannot undo our past, but we can choose the direction in life we will take going forward. *Rahab the harlot* became Rahab the woman of faith … and ultimately Rahab the mother of Boaz, David and Jesus!

Ruth reminds us of the importance of commitment. Ruth came from a nation under a curse, yet she made a commitment to be faithful to her mother-in-law in spite of the personal consequences in her own life. God honored her commitment by bringing her into contact with Boaz—a man of courage and commitment in his own right who understood from his family background how difficult life could be for a woman from another culture.

God honored Ruth's commitment, and later in Isaiah 56 God promised to accept all those who come to Him, no matter what their previous background might be.

Bathsheba, the unnamed woman in the genealogy, reminds us of God's grace and forgiveness. By identifying her as "she of Uriah," Matthew did remind us of her and David's sin—and the awful consequences that came from their actions. But her importance to the line of David, through the birth of her son Solomon, was also intended to remind us of the forgiveness God extends to those who confess their sin.

And, finally, ***Mary*** reminds us that those who choose to follow God will sometimes experience pain, hardship, ridicule and even persecution because of their decision. As Jesus reminded His disciples, "If they persecuted Me, they will also persecute you" (John 15:20).

So, do not be surprised if your love for God is misunderstood ... or rejected ... or even attacked. Mary was the purest of the women in the genealogy of Jesus ... and was probably the one most maligned by those who could not accept the reality that her pregnancy fulfilled God's promise of a virgin giving birth to Immanuel!

Five Golden Rings. Five very different women. Five very practical lessons for us today.

My closing prayer is that God will use the lives of these amazing women to make a difference in your life today!

Dispensational Publishing House is striving to become the go-to source for Bible-based materials from the dispensational perspective.

Our goal is to provide high-quality doctrinal and worldview resources that make dispensational theology accessible to people at all levels of understanding.

Visit our blog regularly to read informative articles from both known and new writers.

And please let us know how we can better serve you.

Dispensational Publishing House, Inc.
PO Box 3181
Taos, NM 87571

Call us toll free 844-321-4202

www.ingramcontent.com/pod-product-compliance
Lightning Source LLC
Chambersburg PA
CBHW071755080526
44588CB00013B/2244